Looking after Gran

Roderick Hunt • Alex Brychta

OXFORD
UNIVERSITY PRESS

The family was going away.
"Look after Floppy," said Dad.

Gran liked looking after Floppy.
She took him for lots of walks.

She threw sticks for him to
chase and balls for him to catch.

Gran had a motorbike.

It was bright red.

"Jump in, Floppy," said Gran.

Gran put on her crash helmet.

"Where are we going?"
thought Floppy.

Soon, they were zooming
into town.
"Isn't this fun!" said Gran.

"Not for me!" thought Floppy.

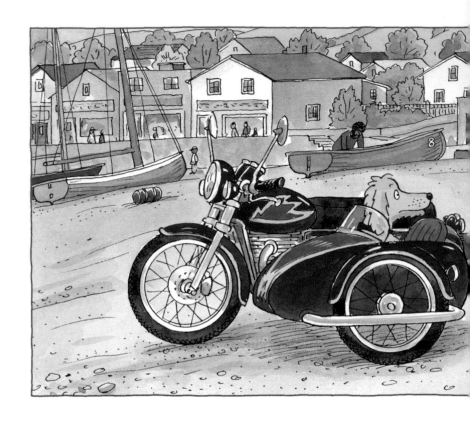

At last, Gran stopped. She parked
the motorbike on the sand.

"Stay here, Floppy," said Gran.
"Look after the motorbike. I'm
going shopping."

Gran was away for a long time.
The tide started to come in. A wave
splashed the front wheel.

Then a wave splashed the back wheel.

"Gran has parked too close to the sea!" thought Floppy.

"I must find Gran," thought
Floppy.

He ran into the town as fast
as he could.

Sniff! Sniff! went Floppy.

He could tell where Gran
had been. She had been in the
butcher's shop.

"Yum! Bones," thought Floppy.

"Get out!" yelled the butcher. "No dogs in here!"

Floppy ran back into
the street.

"I must find Gran," he
thought.

Sniff! Sniff! went Floppy.

Gran had been in the bread shop.

"Get out!" yelled the baker. "No dogs in here!"

Floppy ran back into
the street.
"I must find Gran,"
he thought.

Then Floppy saw Gran.
She was in the hat shop.
Floppy ran in and barked.

"Get out!" said the lady. "No dogs in here!"

"Come on, Gran!" thought Floppy.

Floppy ran out of the shop.
Gran ran after him.

"Come back!" called the lady.
"You haven't paid for that hat."

Floppy ran
back to the beach.
Gran puffed
after him.

"Oh no! My motorbike,"
shouted Gran.

She ran into the sea and pushed
her motorbike out.

"Well done, Floppy," said Gran.
"You saved my motorbike!"

Gran spoke to Mum.

"I'm not looking after Floppy," she said. "He's looking after me!"

Think about the story

Why didn't Floppy like going on Gran's motorbike?

Why did Gran leave Floppy with her motorbike?

Gran told Floppy to stay. Why was he right not to stay?

What animal would you like to look after for a day?

Spot the difference

Find the 10 differences on the motorbikes.

**Useful common words repeated in this story and
other books at Level 4.**

after away back been find get going here looking
must my thought where
Names in this story: Mum Dad Gran Floppy